❄

CHRISTMAS

D. J. HERDA

CHRISTMAS

FRANKLIN WATTS
New York / London / Toronto / Sydney / 1983
A FIRST BOOK

Facing page 1: in Bethlehem, where Christ was born,
crowds fill the Church of the Nativity every Christmas.

Illustrations by Anne Canevari Green

Photographs courtesy of:
Religious News Service:
opp. p. 1, pp. 4, 14, 21, 25, 32;
State Historical Society of Wisconsin:
pp. 27, 38.
Photos on pp. 8, 11, 16, and 50
by Elizabeth McDonald.

Library of Congress Cataloging in Publication Data

Herda, D. J., 1948-
Christmas.

(A First book)
Includes index.
Summary: Briefly describes the history and
traditions of Christmas and celebrations in various parts
of the world. Includes instructions
for making gifts, food, and decorations.
1. Christmas—Juvenile literature.   [1. Christmas]
I. Green, Anne Canevari, ill.   II. Title.
GT4985.H367 1983   394.2'68282   82-15885
ISBN 0-531-04524-2

5

CONTENTS

CHRISTMAS

1

THE HISTORY
OF CHRISTMAS

Christmas. The word brings to mind so many different images. We picture gaily decorated pine trees, brightly wrapped packages, cards wishing friends and relatives good cheer, songs we hear once a year, special foods, parties, religious ceremonies, goodwill, peace, love, and more.

What does Christmas mean and when did it begin? Christmas is basically a Christian holiday that celebrates the birth of Jesus Christ nearly 2,000 years ago. There is little doubt about the year of Christ's birth, but there is some confusion about the exact day He was born.

Today, all Christian churches except the Armenian church observe Christmas on December 25. For over 300 years following Christ's birth no one could agree on one date. In many places throughout the world, His birth was celebrated on January 6. This is the feast of the Epiphany. On this date, Christ was supposed to have been visited by the Magi, or Three Wise

Men, who were among the first to see the infant Jesus. (The Armenian church still celebrates Christmas on January 6.) To make matters even more complicated, the Eastern Christian church preferred celebrating the birth on a "moveable date." This day was determined by observing the movement of the moon from year to year.

We probably owe the setting of December 25 as Christmas to the ancient Romans. The Romans were pagans in the years before the birth of Christ. They worshipped many nature gods—the god of wind, the god of rain, the god of the sun, the god of harvests, etc. For centuries, the Romans celebrated a holiday called *Saturnalia*, or the festival of the *winter solstice*, in December. Each December 22, the earth is tilted at an angle to the sun that gives the Northern Hemisphere the shortest day of the year—the day called the winter solstice. After solstice, the days get longer and longer. Saturnalia was dedicated to the renewed power of the sun, and to Saturn, the god of agriculture.

Saturnalia was a lively, joyful celebration, similar in many ways to our modern Christmas. Great feasts were held in Roman homes. Gifts were exchanged, and everyone was merry.

Following the birth of Christ, the early Christians—the followers of the ways of Jesus Christ—set about converting the pagans to Christianity. By settling on a fixed date for the celebration of the Christian ceremony of Christmas, the early church founders hoped to lure the pagans away from celebrating Saturnalia—the rebirth of the sun—to celebrating the birth of Christ, who was called the "Light of the World."

Of course, the date of December 25 for the celebration of Christmas (the name Christmas comes from the Old English words *Christes Maesee*, or "Christ's Mass") was not accepted overnight. In the year 529, the Roman Emperor, Justinian, declared December 25 a civic holiday. He prohibited work or public business on that day. Then, in the year 567, the Council of Tours, a group of Catholic priests, proclaimed the twelve days from December 25 to Epiphany (January 6) as a sacred season. During these years, both Saturnalia and Christmas were celebrated. But as Catholic missionaries spread the word of Christ's birth throughout the world, more and more people became Christians and celebrated Christmas.

Today, Christmas is still a religious holiday for Roman Catholics, Greeks, Anglicans, Lutherans, and other Christians. In Christian communities throughout the world, Christmas is a day of festivity, of family reunions and joy, and of hope for a prosperous new year. But, above all else, it is the celebration of the birth of Christ. Originally, Christians exchanged greetings during the Christmas season. Soon, they came to exchange gifts, perhaps as a symbol of the Three Wise Men who presented their gifts to the infant Jesus in Bethlehem.

Christmas has become a secular, or nonreligious, holiday, too. Both Christian and non-Christian families exchange presents and offer greetings of peace, hope, and goodwill. In many towns and cities around the world, decorations such as garlands, lights, satin balls, and other festive hangings are put up. Some towns turn their lampposts into giant candy canes by wrapping them with red-and-white paper. And many communities—from the smallest towns to the largest cities—celebrate the season by setting up community Christmas trees in centrally located areas.

Some of these trees are giants much larger than any trees growing in the forests. That is because they are actually made of many dozens of smaller trees lashed together with rope or wire and trimmed so that they look like one huge tree.

*Each year a giant Christmas tree overlooks the
ice-skating rink at New York's Rockefeller Center.*

Other popular community festivities include public gatherings at which Christmas carols and hymns are sung. Everybody sings out joyfully. In some communities, both the choir and the audience, accompanied by a professional orchestra, sing such well-known Christmas pieces as Handel's *Messiah*, one of the most famous Christmas compositions ever written. Songbooks are passed out, and there is a brief rehearsal before the actual performance begins. Thousands of voices sing of the birth of Christ, of goodwill, and of peace on earth.

The nicest thing about Christmas is that peace, love, and good will do not cost a fortune. They are free for the giving! Like the true spirit of Christmas, they come from the heart.

2

THE TRADITIONS
OF CHRISTMAS

Christmas would not be Christmas without many of the traditions that have been passed from generation to generation throughout the ages. And the Christmas tree is one of those traditions.

The first Christmas tree appeared in Germany during the 1500s. But some historians believe it was part of the pagan ceremonies of ancient Rome hundreds of years before.

Nonetheless, by 1604, the Christmas tree was a firmly established tradition in Germany. This tradition spread to Sweden, Norway, and several other Scandinavian and European countries by the 1800s.

In Scandinavia, the tree was considered a sign of good fortune. To this day, many Swedes and Norwegians place small fir trees or boughs on the ridge-poles of newly built homes.

An interesting tale about one of the first Christmas trees concerns Winfred, an English missionary who went to Germany to spread the teachings of Jesus Christ to the pagan Germanic tribespeople. While passing through the woods on Christmas Eve, Winfred stumbled across a group of idol worshipers gathered around a large tree known as the Oak of Geismar. The Germans were preparing to sacrifice Prince Asulf to the pagan god Thor.

Winfred was appalled, and he yelled out to the worshipers. "Stop!" he cried. Then he rushed forward, and with a single stroke from a mighty ax, he felled the oak. As the stunned worshipers looked on, they saw a small fir tree that had been hidden behind the oak. Winfred then told the worshipers that the fir tree was the Tree of Life, a symbol of Jesus Christ. Then he explained the teachings of Jesus. From that moment on, legend has it, the fir tree became both a symbol of Christianity in Germany and the symbol of life throughout much of the rest of the world.

A tradition that was more popular during the colonial period in the United States than it is today is the lighting of the Yule log. In ancient England, it was common belief that the sun stood still for the twelve days at the end of the year (around the time we celebrate Christmas). Fearing that the sun might remain still forever or even "die," the pagans carried a huge log from the woods and placed it in the center of their villages. They lit the log to rekindle the sun and keep it alive. The log was large enough to burn for twelve days, and during that time it was thought to chase away all the evils of the past year.

The practice of lighting the Yule log was adopted by Christians, and it has been a treasured part of Christmas tradition in many countries around the world ever since.

You might not think that mince pie, a holiday treat, is a Christmas tradition, but it is. The practice of preparing this special pie has existed nearly as long as Christmas, itself. The

pie, filled with rich and exotic spices and fruits, represents the treasures that the Three Wise Men brought to the Christ Child in the stable. It was originally baked in the shape of a loaf, resembling the manger in which Christ lay.

Mince pie represents wealth and greatness, but plum pudding—another traditional Christmas sweet—represents the exact opposite. It is a symbol of humility. According to legend, a King and his men became lost in the English forest. It was Christmas Eve. The party had planned to be at their destination long before dark, so they had very few provisions with them. Rather than see his men go hungry, the king ordered everything edible to be combined into a single dish that all could share. So the cook mixed flour and potatoes with walnuts, fruits, peels, carrots, and spices. The meal was named plum pudding, after its main ingredient. Each Christmas Eve thereafter, it became traditional to serve the dish that sustained the king and his men in time of darkness.

Holly, that bright green sprig with the scarlet berries, is another Christmas tradition. It too has many stories behind it. The pagans believed that the evergreen was a promise that the sun would return to the earth and that all things would grow and thrive again after the harshness of winter.

Early Christians, especially the French and English, hung holly over their doors to show that the spirit of Christ lived inside. It is believed that the crown of thorns laid on Jesus' head when He was crucified was wound with the evergreen. It is said that the berries turned from white to red after Christ's death.

The poinsettia is a
popular Christmas flower.

According to a secular tradition, whoever brought the holly into the house at Christmas would rule in the coming year. Imagine the footraces that must have taken place as husbands and wives each tried to outdo each other in being the first to bring the sprig into the house!

Bells have long been a favorite part of Christmas the world over. Ringing the bells on Christmas Eve in medieval times was supposed to warn the devil of the coming birth of Jesus, who would save the world from darkness and sin. For one hour before midnight, the bells would toll. Then, at the stroke of twelve, a triumphant pealing of the bells signaled the birth of the Saviour and the death of the devil.

Did you ever hang a stocking by the mantel in the hopes that Saint Nicholas would fill it with gifts? If so, you were taking part in a holiday tradition that is centuries old.

Saint Nicholas was a bishop in Asia Minor in the fourth century. It is believed that the bishop heard of a poor man who was about to sell his three daughters into slavery because he could no longer afford to keep them. Saint Nicholas saved the three daughters by tossing three sacks of gold down the chimney of the poor man's home. One sack, according to legend, fell into a stocking hanging by the fireplace to dry. Since then, children all over the world have put out their stockings in the hope that Saint Nick would leave them a present.

Christmas cards are another holiday custom. Long ago, people sent private, handwritten notes of good cheer and happiness for the coming year.

Finding the stockings
filled by Saint Nicholas . . .

In the nineteenth century, British students were required to prepare and mail handsome and detailed scrolls of goodwill. Sending the scrolls served two purposes. The students took part in the tradition of sending holiday greetings, and their work showed their teachers how well each of them had learned the fine art of calligraphy (lettering), composition, and art.

It was not until 1843 that the first commercial Christmas card was produced. In that year, Sir Henry Cole arranged to have an illustrator design a card especially for Christmas. It was printed by a method known as lithography and was colored by hand.

One thousand cards were sold that first Chirstmas. Since then, billions of Christmas cards have been sent to express good cheer and hope for the coming year, as well as to help people stay in touch with family and friends living far away.

3

CHRISTMAS AROUND THE WORLD

Nearly every country in the world has its own Christmas legends and its own unique way of celebrating the holiday.

In many Austrian cities, for example, it is common to keep the Christmas tree, usually a fir or pine, locked in a room and out of sight until Christmas Eve. The parents then sneak in to decorate the tree with silver and gold garlands and as many candles as possible. After dinner on Christmas Eve, the father gathers the family around and reads the story of the *Christkind*, or the Christ Child. Then a bell is rung and the door is unlocked and thrown open to reveal the magnificent tree in all its blazing glory!

Presents are spread out beneath the tree. Then the family sings Christmas carols, such as "Silent Night," "O Tannenbaum," and other Austrian favorites.

On Christmas in the Austrian Alps, the mountaineer who lives highest up the mountainside lights a torch and makes his

way slowly down to the home of his nearest neighbor. He is joined by the members of his neighbor's household, who also bear lighted torches.

The mountain dwellers continue down the mountainside, adding more people and more torches along the way. As they travel, the Austrians sing Christmas carols to proclaim that Christ is the messenger of peace and the light of the world. Once they reach the village below, they proceed to the church, where Christmas services begin.

In the Scandinavian country of Denmark, a traditional game is played at the Christmas Eve dinner. The hosts hide a single almond in the rice pudding. The person who finds the almond keeps the discovery a secret until all of the others have finished eating their pudding. Then the lucky person reveals the almond and claims his or her reward, which is usually a candied marzipan. The dinner continues, and a goose stuffed with apples and prunes is served alongside red cabbage, potatoes, and lingonberry sauce.

In Italy, Christmas is a very holy holiday. To celebrate the birth of Jesus, a *presepio*, or manger, is created in nearly every home.

The manger scene was first recreated by Saint Francis of Assisi. In the Italian village of Greccio in 1223, Saint Francis used real animals and villagers to create a "live" manger scene, so that the villagers would know what the birth of Jesus was like.

The practice of constructing miniature Nativity scenes ("Nativity" means the birth of Jesus) spread from Italy into

A Christmas procession
in France

A Nativity scene

many other lands over the years. Eventually, the Nativity inspired artists and craftspeople to make miniature scenes for their homes and the homes of friends. The custom of creating miniature Nativity scenes then spread to royalty, as nobles and kings hired artists to produce the most lavish scenes imaginable.

Although Christmas in Italy is mainly a time devoted to prayer, families do enjoy one festive tradition. Following church services on Christmas Day, each family gathers around a large ornamental bowl called the Urn of Fate. Every family member takes a turn reaching in for a wrapped present until all are distributed. Many of the presents are empty boxes, so that everyone usually gets a "blank" before finally getting a gift. The blanks add to the suspense and fun of the event.

Christmas in the Soviet Union has a rich heritage. One tradition, for example, mixed both pagan and Christian rituals. A young maiden was dressed in white to represent the goddess of the sun. She was then drawn from house to house in a sleigh while several other maidens sang Christmas carols.

The day after Christmas was reserved for the men of the village to go visiting. The women paid their respects the next day.

Fortune-telling has played a large role in the Soviet Union's Christmas traditions over the years. Some Russians believe they can predict the future by "reading" a drop of molten lead splattered on the snow. Another even more intriguing custom exists. The young women of a family make five small piles of grain on the floor of the kitchen. Each pile is said to signify something for the future, such as wealth, health, happiness, marriage, or poverty. At midnight, a sleeping hen is taken from the roost and brought into the home. As the hen gradually becomes used to the bright lights and laughing people, it eventually sees and smells the grain and walks over to peck at one pile. The pile chosen by the hen is supposed to indicate the future of the maiden whose fortune is being told.

Sweden, too, is a country rich in the heritage of Christmas. In pagan times, many Swedes believed that trolls, goblins, and witches walked the villages in search of dark corners in which to dwell and do their dirty deeds undetected. Thus, every Christmas season, Swedish families cleaned their homes completely. Every corner and every cupboard would be made spotless. It was better to toil all day, Swedish women believed, than to host these demons by night!

Of course, the Swedes have long been known for their excellent foods and sweets. At midday on Christmas Eve, young and old alike gather in the kitchen to partake of *doppa i grytan,* or "dip-in-the-pot." On the stove, a large kettle of broth simmers. When it is done, each member of the family takes a piece of special rye bread, dips it into the pot, and eats it. The custom is supposed to remind the family members that all food is precious, no matter how simple.

No one eats too much of dip-in-the-pot, though, for everyone knows that Christmas Eve dinner is coming. In the evening, friends and family settle down to the largest Christmas ham to be found. Accompanying the ham are two traditional Swedish dishes—*lutefisk* and rice pudding. *Lutefisk,* a sundried, lime-cured fish, is popular food in Scandinavian countries. The smell of cooking *lutefisk* is the very smell of Christmas in most Swedish homes.

Rice pudding is also a Swedish holiday tradition. As in Denmark, the pudding contains a single almond. Before eating the pudding, everyone must make up a rhyme. Then, whoever ends up with the hidden almond is supposed to be married by the next Christmas. Of course, if a *married* person gets the almond, it is thought there will be no marriages in the family during the coming year.

Christmas in Finland begins long before December 25. In fact, the Finns celebrate the last Sunday in November, which they call "Little Christmas," as the beginning of the holiday season. Giant Christmas trees go up for sale in marketplaces all over the cities and villages. Stores bring out all their holiday decorations. At home, Finns gather for parties, songs, and feasting. They especially enjoy eating homemade gingerbread snaps and the first sampling of the Christmas pudding, which is consumed throughout the Christmas season.

Traditionally, on Christmas Eve, the Finns visit their saunas. These are bathhouses where stones are heated until red hot. Then cold water is poured over the stones to produce steam, which swells to every corner of the room. As the Finns soak up the heat and steam, they dream about the great meal of porridge, fish, and other Finnish delights which they will soon consume.

After dinner, the Finns gather around the Christmas tree to await the arrival of Santa Claus, who, according to Finnish legend, arrives early in the evening from distant Lapland. Then, after exchanging presents, everyone retires early in order to be ready for Christmas church services, which start promptly at 7 A.M. Christmas Day.

When December 26 arrives, the holiday celebration is still going strong, for that is Saint Stephen's Day. It is marked by the traditional Saint Stephen's Day horseraces along snowy country roads. In the afternoon and evening, relatives and friends visit and often dance.

In England, a country rich in the traditions of Christmas, blazing plum pudding, a crackling Yule log, and rosy-cheeked carolers are symbols of holiday cheer. One of the oldest English Christmas foods is mince pie. A recipe dated 1344 calls for the chopped meat of pheasants, hares, and partridges instead of the modern equivalents of chopped beef and suet.

In the 1400s, King Henry VII introduced England to the wassail bowl from the Scandinavian countries. The wassail bowl is large bowl containing a mixture of hot ale, spices, and toasted apples. A drink of good cheer, it is shared by family and friends during the holidays as an omen of success for the coming year. In some places, beehives, trees, and fields are still wassailed, or toasted, to insure prosperous harvests.

In northern regions, sleigh bells, snow, and frost-covered windows are part of Christmas. But that is not at all what Christmas is like in Brazil. This South American country celebrates Christmas during its summer season, so many of the Portuguese, Italian, German, Polish, English, American, and Japanese people who have settled in Brazil celebrate Christmas by going to the beaches.

The typical Brazilian home has a manger scene, which is set up early in December. Each day, the three figures of the Wise Men are moved closer to the manger. On Christmas Eve, the infant Jesus, which has been kept hidden, is placed in the crib.

Presents are exchanged in Brazilian homes on Christmas Eve, and then families gather around their trees and sing car-

Las Posadas celebration in Tucson, Arizona, where the Mexican community carries on the old traditions. The children chant, "Who will give shelter?"

ols. The Day of the Three Kings is also an important Christmas season celebration. Then, children set out their shoes into which presents will be placed, symbolizing the visit of the Wise Men to the baby, Jesus.

In Mexico, Christmas arrives without snow but with many festivities. On December 16, Mexicans decorate their homes with flowers, evergreens, and colored paper lanterns. Then, Nativity scenes are set up.

At the same time, Mexicans take part in traditional house visits. Groups of people go from door to door. They carry candles and chant a song asking for shelter. At each house, they are told there is no room. The search continues until Christmas Eve. This custom is called *Las Posadas*, which means "resting places" in Spanish. It honors and re-enacts the journey that Mary and Joseph took when they were traveling the countryside in search of shelter.

On Christmas Eve, the pilgrims on these house visits finally find a home in which the innkeeper has room. This symbolizes the fact that Joseph and Mary were finally given shelter in a stable, where Jesus was born. Then everyone in the home kneels before an altar with a Nativity scene and prays.

After prayers, the Mexicans have a party complete with singing, dancing, and game playing. A *piñata*, a large earthenware jar, is filled with candy, fruit, nuts, and small gifts. The pot may be decorated as a clown's face, a bull, or some other design.

After the *piñata* is hung by a long rope from the ceiling, the children at the party are blindfolded, turned around a few times, and given three chances to break the *piñata* by swinging at it with a stick. When someone finally cracks it and the prizes inside spill onto the floor, everyone rushes about wildly to claim a present.

Christmas in Puerto Rico features many American customs, but there are a number of Latin American traditions observed there, too. Groups of *trullas*, or carol singers, travel the countryside at Christmastime. Sometimes they walk, sometimes they travel by horseback, and sometimes they go by car. Often they are repaid for their songs with food and drink.

Christians in the United States observe many of the same customs as Christians around the world. But we have our own special traditions, too.

Most people in the United States have never seen a blazing Yule log and would not know a wassail punch from a bowl of eggnog. But almost all Christians enjoy traditions that have been borrowed from other countries. Some customs are the holiday wreath, caroling, mistletoe, exchanging cards and presents, and, of course, decorating a Christmas tree.

The Christmas tree is an important part of the holiday in the United States. Trees are cut early and shipped from one end of the country to the other. This way, everyone has an opportunity to buy one. Some people prefer cutting their own trees, and there are lots of do-it-yourself tree farms for that purpose. Armed with a small tree saw and plenty of enthusiasm, thousands of Americans set out in search of the "perfect" tree.

Once the tree is brought home, it is usually set up in a stand containing a water-and-sugar solution to preserve it. Then the holiday tradition of decorating the tree begins. Decorations vary widely, from ornate and colorful satin bows, balls, and ribbons to the more traditional "country Christmas" decorations of strings of popcorn and cranberries, candy canes, garlands, and homemade ornaments. A star or angel is usually placed on the very top of the tree. The star represents the Star of Bethlehem that shone over the manger, and the angel represents the angel who showed the world where Jesus lay.

4

THE MUSIC OF
CHRISTMAS

Singing is a way to express many feelings. Therefore, what could be more natural than singing joyful carols and songs about Christmas, Christ, and the holiday season?

Many of the Christmas songs we enjoy today were written so long ago that we can only guess at their origins. Some were probably ancient pagan chants sung long before Christ was born. They were probably adapted for Christian worship.

Some of the carols and songs we know and love began as folk songs, pastorals (songs of shepherds), or lullabies. They are simple melodies and make lovely Christmas songs.

Several countries have claimed to be the birthplace of the Christmas carol, but no one is actually sure where carols originated. We do know that carols have been part of the church Christmas festivities since the very beginning of Christianity.

The word "carol" probably comes from the Greek *choros*, which means a dance. Until the fourteenth century, the word "carol" was often used to refer to a song people danced to.

Today, when we think of Christmas carols, we often think of groups of people walking from house to house to sing a few songs and accept some hot chocolate and cookies or a contribution to a charity. Or we may think of the carols sung at religious services in the churches at which we worship.

Not very long ago, caroling was forbidden in churches. Even today, many churches do not have caroling until Christmas Eve. The church season of Advent, which is the period beginning four Sundays before Christmas, is seen by some Christians as a time of somber prayer, meditation, and waiting for the birth of Christ.

In the past, caroling was allowed only out-of-doors. To this day, groups of singers called "waits" continue the ancient custom of making the rounds on Christmas Eve in England. The waits sing outside doors and windows and receive gifts of goods and money from their audiences inside.

In the country of Wales, carolers make their rounds at dawn to awaken the villagers to the glorious morning of Christmas. In France, carolers, known as *noels*, sing in the streets of the largest cities and the smallest hamlets. And in the countryside in Italy, shepherds still walk from house to house, singing carols to the accompaniment of bagpipelike instruments.

One of the most interesting caroling customs originated in the country of Rumania. There, a Star of Bethlehem is constructed, decorated with frills and bells, and carried by carolers who travel from house to house. The star is created by making a five-sided box. The front and back are covered with paper. On each paper, a picture of the Virgin Mary or some other religious subject is painted. A candle is placed within the box to illuminate the pictures from behind. Then the star is placed atop a tall pole and carried by the singers.

*Christmas morning carols by
children in Yorkshire, England*

Many of the world's most popular Christmas carols originated as religious hymns. Here are a few of the most popular carols of all times.

ADESTES FIDELES
(OH COME, ALL YE FAITHFUL)

Originally a Latin hymn of praise, this song was composed by John Reading in the 1700s. It first appeared in a collection of songs known as *Cantus Diversi* in 1751. Many English translations have been made over the years, but the most familiar is this one, by Frederick Oakley.

> *Oh come, all ye faithful, joyful and triumphant,*
> *Oh come, ye, Oh come, ye, to Bethlehem;*
> *Come and behold Him, born the King of Angels,*
> *Oh come let us adore Him,*
> *Oh come let us adore Him,*
> *Oh come let us adore Him, Christ, the Lord.*

HARK! THE HERALD ANGELS SING!

Charles Wesley, an English preacher and hymn writer, composed the words to this popular Christmas carol in 1739. Originally, the carol began, "Hark, how all the welkin rings," but the words were changed to the more familiar ones over the years. The melody is from the *Festgesänge* by the German composer, Felix Mendelssohn.

> *Hark! the herald angels sing,*
> *"Glory to the newborn King;*
> *Peace on earth and mercy mild,*
> *God and sinners reconciled!"*
> *Joyful all ye nations rise,*
> *Join the triumph of the skies;*

With th' angelic host proclaim,
"Christ is born in Bethlehem!"
Hark, the herald angels sing,
"Glory to the newborn King!"

JOY TO THE WORLD

Isaac Watts, the English hymn writer, based this jubilant carol on the Ninety-eighth Psalm from the Bible. Its words reflect the typical missionary spirit present in Britain during the early 1700s. Lowell Mason, an early American composer, arranged the words to several choruses from the oratorio the *Messiah*, by German-born composer George Frideric Handel.

Joy to the world! the Lord is come;
Let earth receive her King;
Let every heart prepare Him room.
And heaven and nature sing,
And heaven and nature sing,
And heaven and heaven and nature sing.

O COME, O COME, EMMANUEL

This carol was taken from a short verse which was originally sung in Latin in the Roman Catholic Church during vespers (evening worship) just before Christmas. John Mason Neale translated it. The tune was adapted from a song of the 1200s.

O come, O come, Emmanuel,
And ransom captive Israel;
That mourns in lonely exile here,
Until the Son of God appear.
Rejoice! Rejoice!
Emmanuel shall come to thee,
Come to thee, O Israel!

GOD REST YE,
MERRY GENTLEMEN

This popular carol dates back to the 1800s, but its origins are unknown. A favorite in England, it is similar to many older carols.

God rest ye, merry gentlemen:
Let nothing you dismay.
For Jesus Christ, our Savior,
Was born on Christmas Day.
To save us all from Satan's power
When we were gone astray.
O tidings of comfort and joy,
Comfort and joy.
O tidings of comfort and joy!

O LITTLE TOWN
OF BETHLEHEM

The words to this carol were written by Phillips Brooks, a well-known Boston minister. He wrote them in 1867 for his Sunday school class in Philadelphia, where he was preaching at the time. Lewis Redner, the organist of the church, set the words to music.

O little town of Bethlehem,
How still we see thee lie!
Above thy deep and dreamless sleep
The silent stars go by;
Yet in the dark streets shineth
The everlasting light;
The hopes and fears of all the years
Are met in thee tonight.

SILENT NIGHT, HOLY NIGHT!

One of the most well-known and best-loved carols in the world, this song was written by Joseph Mohr, a pastor in Oberndorf, Austria, in the nineteenth century. According to legend, Mohr was upset because the church organ had broken down and could not be repaired in time for that night's Christmas Eve services.

Mohr went for a walk in the countryside, wondering what he would do for music. When he returned, he scribbled down the lyrics to "Silent Night." Franz Gruber, the schoolmaster, composed the tune and accompanied Mohr on the guitar that very night.

Silent Night, Holy Night!
All is calm, all is bright,
'Round yon Virgin Mother and Child,
Holy Infant so tender and mild.
Sleep in heavenly peace,
Sleep in heavenly peace.

THE FIRST NOEL

This one is a mystery, because no one is quite sure who wrote it. We do know that it appeared in 1833 in *Christmas Carols Ancient and Modern*, collected by W. B. Sandys.

The first Noel, the angel did say,
Was to certain poor shepherds in fields as they lay;
In fields where they lay keeping their sheep,
On a cold winter's night that was so deep.
Noel, Noel, Noel, Noel,
Born is the King of Israel.

Saint Nicholas Church in Oberndorf, Austria,
where "Silent Night" was sung for the first time.

IT CAME UPON
A MIDNIGHT CLEAR

Edmund H. Sears wrote the words to this Christmas hymn in 1849. At the time, he was pastor of a church in Wayland, Massachusetts. The music was written by Richard S. Willis, who was then editor of *Musical World*.

> *It came upon a midnight clear,*
> *That glorious song of old,*
> *From angels bending near the earth*
> *To touch their harps of gold;*
> *"Peace on the earth, goodwill to men,*
> *From heaven's all-gracious King";*
> *The world in solemn stillness lay,*
> *To hear the angels sing.*

WHILE SHEPHERDS
WATCHED THEIR FLOCKS

Nahum Tate, a British dramatist and poet, wrote this composition in 1703. It is based upon a familiar melody taken from *Siroe*, an opera by George Frideric Handel.

> *While shepherds watched their flocks by night,*
> *All seated on the ground,*
> *The angel of the Lord came down*
> *And glory shone around;*
> *And glory shone around.*

WHAT CHILD IS THIS?

William C. Dix wrote the words to this carol in the late 1800s. The tune is an old English song known as *Greensleeves*.

What child is this, who, laid to rest
On Mary's lap is sleeping?
Whom angels greet with anthems sweet,
While shepherds watch are keeping.
This, this is Christ the King,
Whom shepherds guard and angels sing:
Haste, haste, to bring Him laud,
The Babe, the Son of Mary.

GO TELL IT ON THE MOUNTAIN

This is a modern American addition to the world's Christmas
carols. It is a Negro spiritual, originally sung by black slaves on
Southern cotton plantations. It passed from one plantation to
the next and survived by oral tradition, or word of mouth.

When I was a seeker, I sought both night and day,
I sought the Lord to help me, and He showed me the way,
He made me a watchman up on the city wall,
And if I am a Christian, I am the least of all.
CHORUS
Oh, go tell it on the mountain,
Over the hills and everywhere,
Go tell it on the mountain that
Jesus Christ is born!

Of course, not all Christmas songs are based on religious
hymns of praise. Some, especially the more recent ones, are
secular, or nonreligious. Of these, one of the most popular ever
written was by the American composer Irving Berlin. It is entitled "White Christmas." This song is one of the most widely
known and best-loved of the more than 900 creations by Berlin.

"White Christmas" was written for the film *Holiday Inn*, produced in Hollywood in 1942. The movie, made by Paramount Pictures, starred Bing Crosby and Fred Astaire.

After Crosby sang the song in the movie, it became an instant hit and earned Berlin an Academy Award as the Best Song of 1942. "White Christmas" helped boost the morale of thousands of American soldiers fighting in the jungles and swamps of the Pacific during World War II. Its Christmas images and Yuletide messages of peace and good cheer brought those soldiers a little bit of home.

Since its introduction, a record-breaking 4 million copies of sheet music and more than 100 million sound recordings of the song have been sold.

According to a recent poll taken by George Gallup, "White Christmas" is now second only to the carol "Silent Night" as America's favorite Christmas song. It was also the basis for a movie entitled *White Christmas* that was made some years after *Holiday Inn*. Here are the words to "White Christmas."

I'm dreaming of a white Christmas,
Just like the ones I used to know,
Where the treetops glisten and children listen
To hear sleigh bells in the snow.
I'm dreaming of a white Christmas
With every Christmas card I write.
May your days be merry and bright,
And may all your Christmases be white.

5

CHRISTMAS GIFTS

Giving gifts to friends and loved ones during the Christmas season is a tradition that dates back centuries. In fact, it probably dates all the way back to the very first Christmas, when the Three Kings came to Bethlehem and presented gifts to the infant Jesus. People have been giving gifts on Christmas ever since.

In the United States, gifts are usually exchanged on Christmas Eve or Christmas Day. However, in many other countries, presents are given on January 6. This date is the Twelfth Night of Christmas, called the Epiphany. It was the date on which the Three Kings visited the Christ Child. Thus, people in Poland, Italy, Spain, and other nations celebrate this day and reserve it for their gift-giving.

Did you know that many people throughout the world also used to exchange gifts on December 6? It has nothing to do with Christ's birth, but rather with someone's death. On

December 6, in the year A.D. 345, Nicholas, the kind bishop who lived in Asia Minor, died. People respected and admired Nicholas so much that they began exchanging gifts in his memory. And that is how the celebration called Saint Nicholas Day was born. Many people still exchange small tokens of love and respect on that day.

Over the years, Saint Nicholas Day and Christmas merged, and Saint Nicholas—or St. Nick, for short—became the patron saint of December 25. And the people of the world had one more reason for exchanging gifts on Christmas.

Christmas is a celebration of joy and love, of peace, kindness, and humility. On that day everyone can give gifts to those they love. No matter how old you are or how much money you have in your piggy bank, you can give a truly wonderful present on Christmas.

Did you ever stop to think about what you would give your parents for Christmas if you had all the money in the world? Theater tickets? A big, beautiful art book? A new toaster? How about a stove? Or a new fuel-efficient car? Or even a new *house?*

Those gifts might be nice. But there are other gifts that would be even nicer. There are some gifts your parents will cherish for a lifetime, gifts that money cannot buy. They are absolutely free, or they cost just pennies. They are gifts of the heart—gifts that show how much you love someone and how much you care. Here are a couple of examples.

GIFTS OF YOURSELF

These gifts come from *you*, not from a store.

1. Tell your parents you love them, and tell them *why*. Telling them on Christmas will make the day extra special.

2. Volunteer to do a chore you do not particularly enjoy doing. For example, you might offer to take out the garbage for a week, shovel snow, keep your room spotless for a month, set the table, or babysit for your younger brother or sister.

3. Find a piece of paper and some crayons or markers. Then draw a picture of the family at Christmas. Roll the drawing into a cylinder, tie a ribbon or string around it, and place it under the tree.

4. Make your own Christmas card. Take a sheet of construction paper or typing paper and fold it in half to resemble a card. Then search through old, discarded magazines and newspapers for pictures to cut out and paste or tape to your card. (Be sure to use magazines and newspapers that no one wants anymore.) You might find a picture of a sleigh cutting through a snow-covered forest to paste on the front. Then cut out a favorite Christmas poem or write your own poem or message on the inside. Attach a string to the card, and hang it from the tree for your parents to find on Christmas morning.

5. Make a special photo card. If you have a favorite photograph, perhaps one of your family, you can make a personalized photo card. Take a sheet of construction paper and fold it in half. Then fold it again in the opposite direction so that it resembles a card. Next, cut a circle in the front, from the first layer of paper. Cut it just smaller than the size of the snapshot to go inside the card. Slip the photo between the two layers of

Saint Nicholas Day
celebration in Holland

paper that form the front of the card. The picture should just peek out through the cutout circle. Secure the photo with tape and write a special message inside.

6. Make a stained-glass ornament or window decoration. Start with a large piece of construction paper or an 8-inch by 10-inch (20-cm by 25-cm) sheet of cardboard. Then, using a lead pencil, draw the shape of your ornament on it. Perhaps you would like it to be a bell, a star, or an angel. Once you have drawn the outline of the figure you want, cut the ornament out along the pencil line. Then draw a second line on the card-board -sheet or construction paper, all the way around your cut-out figure, about 1 inch (2.5 cm) from the edges. Stick a sharpened pencil through the card or paper on this line, and, carefully using scissors, begin cutting along the pencil line from that starter hole. Continue until you have cut out and removed the entire "frame" of the ornament.

Next, take a sheet of waxed paper slightly larger than the size of your ornament. Color it with broad-tipped markers. Use different colors. Apply the colors in small blotches, swirls, or whatever design you like. If you do not have markers, use crayons.

Once you have finished "staining" your waxed-paper "glass," put some glue on the back of the ornament frame and press it against the waxed paper so that the colors show through the cut-out section of the figure. Allow it to dry well. Then trim off any "edges" of waxed paper showing outside the edges of the ornament. Finally, using a sharp pencil, punch a small hole at the top of the ornament, and attach a pipe cleaner or piece of string through the hole as a hanger. Hang your ornament in a sunny window where the light will give it a stained-glass effect, or place it on your tree.

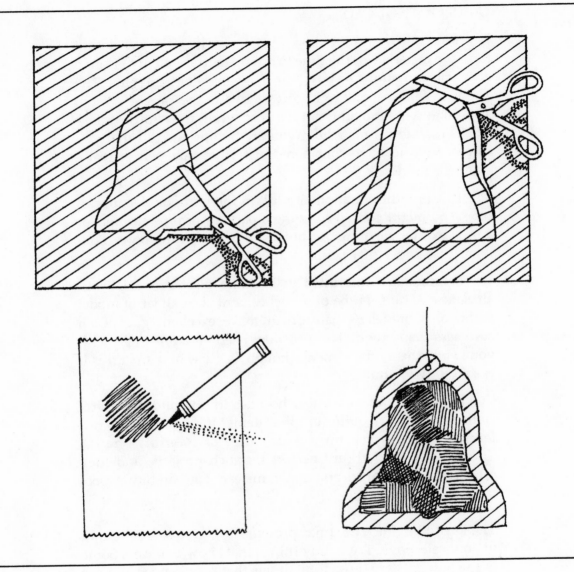

Stained-glass ornament

GIFTS OF THOUGHT

If you do not want to make a Christmas gift, or if you do not have the materials or the time to do so, there are plenty of small gifts you can afford to buy that make excellent presents. The key is to find just the right gift to give to the proper person. This takes some thought. But it is well worth the effort, because it tells the person for whom you are buying the gift that you care enough to have considered just what that person really wants or needs.

If your father or another adult in the household smokes a pipe, you might consider buying a package of pipe cleaners or a pipe tool for cleaning out burned ashes from the bowl. Both items cost under fifty cents.

For someone interested in building plastic model boats, airplanes, or cars, a tube of model cement, a small jar of model paint, or a modeler's paintbrush make excellent gifts. Each costs less than one dollar. You may need an adult to go with you to buy the model cement, though, because in many areas it is sold only to adults.

Do you know someone who likes to sew and make doll clothes, patchwork quilts, or other items? If so, you can go to a fabric shop and pick up a wide range of colorful "scraps." These pieces of cloth are perfect for such projects, and they often cost only pennies apiece. Or, instead, you can buy a spool of thread and a needle.

The key to buying Christmas presents is to give some thought to your selections. Try to buy things that show you care. Some of the best gifts are those little things that people need and use in their everyday lives.

6

FOODS AND FEASTS

When you think of Christmas, it is almost impossible not to think of food. Christmas is a time of celebration, both religious and secular. And celebration means plenty of fabulous food.

Undoubtedly your family has a favorite Christmas menu. Perhaps it is a stuffed Christmas goose, roasted slowly for hours until it is juicy and tender. It might be served with cranberry sauce and candied yams topped with melted marshmallows. Or maybe your family's favorite is a roast turkey and all the trimmings.

All over the world, the holiday season is celebrated with tasty things to eat. But each country has its own specialties, and many of the dishes described in this chapter may be new and interesting.

In many nations, plum pudding is a holiday favorite. It is not like the puddings you may have enjoyed, however. Plum pudding is a unique blend of raisins, citrus-fruit peels, figs, beef suet, spices, mashed potatoes, and many other ingredients, covered with a rich, fragrant sauce.

Another Christmastime favorite in many countries is Yule dough. This is plain pastry formed into flat cakes in the shape of a crib. Mince pies, too, were originally baked to remind us of the fact that Christmas is the celebration of the birth of Christ. They were made into the shape of a manger.

In England, Henry VIII had a taste for what he considered to be the ultimate delicacy—the gently roasted head of a boar, or wild pig.

In France, people to this day enjoy a Christmas meal of turkey, black pudding, strasbourg pie, and spiced gingerbread.

In neighboring Germany, a favorite holiday treat is marzipan. Marzipan, a candy made from crushed almonds, sugar, and egg whites, is made into all sorts of shapes and colors. They are made to resemble everything from fowl, hams, bananas, and apples to celery, radishes, and cucumbers.

Italians celebrate the holiday with Magi cakes, fried eels from the Mediterranean Sea, fresh melons, wine, chicken, and pork with mustard sauce.

In Spain, the feasting is somewhat simpler with fowl, fruit, and wine.

Regardless of what your own family's Christmas favorites may be, it is fun to experiment with different foods during the holidays. There are thousands of recipes just for Christmas. And many of them are simple to make and delightful to eat.

If *you* get the urge to test your creativity in the kitchen, here are a few holiday recipes you may enjoy. But one word of caution: be careful. Never operate electrical appliances such as blenders, mixers, or food processors without adult supervision, because they can be dangerous. Do *not* use the stove or other heating appliances without an adult present.

PARTY CHEESE LOG

1/2 cup chopped walnuts or almonds
4 ounces blue or Roquefort cheese
8-ounce package of cream cheese
1/4 teaspoon garlic salt
1 tablespoon chopped green pepper or chives
1 tablespoon pimento

Heat the oven to 350°. Spread the walnuts or almonds in a shallow pan and toast them, stirring occasionally to prevent them from burning (probably about 8 to 10 minutes). Melt the cheeses together and stir in the garlic salt, pimento, and green pepper or chives. Chill the mixture for several hours until it is firm; then shape it into a log. Roll the cheese log in the toasted nuts and chill it again until serving time. If you like, you may garnish the log with a sprig of holly and serve the cheese with different kinds of thin crackers.

CHRISTMAS COOKIES

3 cups all-purpose flour
1 teaspoon baking powder
3/4 teaspoon salt
1 tablespoon milk
1/2 cup shortening
1 1/2 cups sugar
2 eggs
1 1/2 teaspoons vanilla

Sift the flour to yield 3 cups. Add baking powder and salt, and sift again. Cream the shortening and sugar together until they are light and fluffy. Add the eggs one at a time, beating well. Stir in the vanilla and milk. Add the dry ingredients, and mix them until they are well blended. Wrap the dough in waxed paper and chill it in the refrigerator for about 2 hours. On a lightly floured board, roll out the dough until it is 1/8 inch (.3 cm) thick. Cut the dough into Christmas shapes with cookie cutters. Bake the cookies on a greased cookie sheet in a medium oven (375°) for 8 to 10 minutes. Be careful not to burn them! Cool them on a rack.

CANDY CANE COOKIES

Get all of the above ingredients, plus
1/2 teaspoon red food coloring and
1 teaspoon imitation peppermint.

Make the Christmas Cookie dough, as above. But before chilling the dough, divide it in half, and add 1/2 teaspoon red food coloring and 1 teaspoon imitation peppermint (more or less, to taste) to the other half. When chilled, pinch off pieces of dough and roll each piece into ropelike strips 6 inches (15 cm) in length and about 1/2 inch (1.3 cm) thick. To make candy canes, lay a red and a white strip next to each other. Starting in the middle, twist the two strips together. Then bend one end to resemble a cane. Bake them in the oven at about 375° for 8 to 10 minutes. Serve them with hot chocolate.

PEANUT BUTTER BALLS

1 cup raisins
1/2 cup peanut butter
1/2 cup confectioners sugar
1/4 teaspoon cinnamon
2 tablespoons lemon juice
shredded coconut

Mince the raisins into small pieces. Mix them with 1/2 cup peanut butter and 1/2 cup confectioners sugar. Stir in the cinnamon and the lemon juice. Form the dough into small balls. Roll each ball in shredded coconut and then chill. The recipe yields about 30 small balls.

ROLLED COOKIE FACES

3 1/2 cups flour
1 teaspoon salt
1 cup butter or margarine
1 cup sugar
2 eggs
1 teaspoon vanilla
chocolate chips

Sift the flour and salt together to yield 3 1/2 cups. Beat together 1 cup butter (or margarine) and 1 cup sugar. When this mixture is fluffy, beat in the 2 eggs, vanilla, and the sifted flour and salt. Wrap the dough in waxed paper and chill it overnight. The next day, roll the dough out to about 1/8-inch (.3-cm) thick. Cut it into 2-inch (5-cm) circles, using a round cookie cutter or the mouth of a glass. Place the circles on an ungreased cookie sheet. Add chocolate-chip faces (two chips for the eyes, one for the nose, and several for a smiling mouth.) Bake the cookies in the oven at 375° for 10 minutes.

CHRISTMAS MINTS

3 egg whites
6 cups confectioners sugar
food coloring
various mint extracts

In a large mixing bowl, beat 3 egg whites until stiff. (This takes a long time. Have an adult or an older sister or brother help you beat the egg whites.) Slowly blend in 6 cups sifted confectioners sugar. Divide the candy into three bowls. Tint one mixture red, one green, and one yellow. Flavor each with one of three different mint extracts, such as spearmint, peppermint, and wintergreen. Roll each mixture out between pieces of waxed paper. Cut them into patties with a circular cookie cutter or the mouth of a glass. Let them dry overnight.

SUGAR-FROSTED FRUIT

white of 1 egg, beaten
sugar
apricots
prunes

Dip little clusters of dried apricots and prunes into the beaten egg white. Drain off the excess egg white, and dip the clusters in confectioners sugar. Place them on paper towels to dry, and arrange the fruits on a platter.

FROSTED STUFFED FIGS

dried figs
whole almonds or halved walnuts
confectioners sugar

Slit one side of a whole dried fig and fill the center with walnuts or almonds. Press the fig closed, and dip the bottom of the fig into sifted confectioners sugar. Repeat to make as many frosted stuffed figs as you like.

ORANGE-CRANBERRY PUNCH

Mix one quart cranberry juice, one 6-ounce can of frozen orange juice, one 28-ounce bottle of ginger ale, and 1/4 teaspoon each of salt, nutmeg, cinnamon, allspice, and cloves. Pour this over ice cubes in a punch bowl. Float orange or lemon slices on top. It makes about 12 servings.

FLOATING PUNCH

1 pint vanilla ice cream, softened by standing at room temperature
3/4 teaspoon rum extract
1/3 cup maple syrup
1 quart bottled chocolate milk

Combine the ice cream and rum extract. Put the mixture into an 8-inch (20-cm) jello ring mold and pack firmly. Freeze it until it is solid. "Unmold" the mixture, and place it in a punch bowl. Combine the remaining ingredients. Mix them well, and pour them into a bowl. It makes 10 to 12 servings.

7

DO-IT-YOURSELF
DECORATIONS

There are many, many ways of decorating a home for the holidays—both indoors and out. Why not start thinking of things you can do to make your home look more "Christmasy?" To get you started, here are a few simple suggestions.

CHRISTMAS FOR THE BIRDS

This birds' Christmas tree will bring some of the holiday spirit to your feathered friends and provide you with weeks of fun.

For starters, you will need some sort of tree to decorate outdoors. It can be a small, growing tree, such as an apple tree, a cut Christmas tree, or even the dead branch from a larger oak or maple. If you use a Christmas tree or a branch, stick it in the snow near a window. Or, if the ground is not frozen, open up a slit with a shovel, stick the "tree" in, and pack the ground down again with your heel. The tree should be sturdy enough to stand up under the weight of several "ornaments" and birds.

How do you decorate a tree for birds? Use things the birds will enjoy, such as food. You can make a string of raisins, cranberries, and popcorn. Attach a needle to one end of the string and tie a knot at the other end. Then pierce the yummies with the needle, pull a piece of fruit or popcorn through, and push it down to the knot. Continue stringing in this manner until the entire string is filled.

Get some birdseed, grass seed, or sunflower seed, and mix it with suet (available at most meat counters) or peanut butter. Make small balls from the mixture and place them in the refrigerator to harden. Place these balls in old, throw-away nylon stockings, and tie the tops closed with bright ribbon or yarn. Then cut a vertical slit in the stocking to allow the birds to get at the treat inside. Tie a string around the top of these bird ornaments to fasten them to the branches of your tree.

Once your "bird tree" is fully decorated with raisin strings and suet-seed balls, sit back and watch the fun. It won't take the birds in your neighborhood long to discover your special tree, and you can watch them close up. Once you begin feeding the birds, you must continue to do so throughout the winter. They may come to rely on the food, and if it is no longer available, they may starve.

DOOR STAR

Many people hang balsam or fir wreaths on the outside of their doors at Christmas. But how about a balsam star? You can make one by picking up some evergreen scraps when you go to get your tree. (Often, the scraps are free for the asking.) Trim five of these boughs into the shape of miniature trees, pointed at

Birds' Christmas tree

Door star

one end. Then fasten the five boughs together with sturdy wire (such as a thin clothes hanger) at the blunt or wide ends. The tips should be evenly spaced so that when the five are fastened together they will form the shape of a star.

Decorate your evergreen star with gaily colored Christmas bows or ornaments, and fasten it to the door with heavy-duty nylon tape or tacks.

CHRISTMAS CARD WREATH

Are the Christmas cards your family receives always falling on the floor, behind the couch, or behind a radiator? You can solve that problem and create an interesting holiday decoration at the same time.

Take a wire clothes hanger and bend it so that it forms a circle with the hook on top. Fasten a large red bow or a piece of evergreen just below the hook. Then, when your family's Christmas cards begin to arrive, you can tape them to the wire. Hang the wreath anywhere you like—but remember it will begin getting heavy when it is filled with cards.

CARDBOARD FROSTY

Winter would not be winter without Frosty the Snowman. But it is hard to make a real figure out of snow when there is no snow on the ground. And even if there is, you cannot bring the figure inside!

But you *can* create an indoor snow figure. It is every bit as nice and it won't melt! Start by cutting two or three circles from heavy cardboard. Make each circle larger than the last. Overlap the circles and fasten them together with glue or tape so that the largest circle is on the bottom and the smallest is on the top.

Next, take some white cotton and glue. Using just small amounts at a time, spread a thin coat of glue over the cardboard. Attach the cotton. Cover the entire cardboard figure.

Finally, add the finishing touches to your cardboard snow figure. Use buttons for the eyes, nose, and mouth. If it is a man, you can tape a black construction-paper stovepipe hat to its head. Hang the snow figure from a string, or tape it to the window. Or, if you prefer, use it as a Christmas-tree ornament.

"INSTANT" PAPIER-MÂCHÉ ORNAMENTS

With papier mâché you can make all sorts of Christmas decorations. But papier mâché is sometimes difficult to work with, and it often takes a long time to harden.

Instead of making papier mâché from scratch, you can get a commercial product called *Instant Papier Mâché*®. It is manufactured by the Celluclay Company and is available at paint, hardware, and craft stores.

Put the material in a large mixing bowl, add water, and work it with your fingers until it is moldable. To make Christmas-tree ornaments, pack the sticky material into a mold (a cookie mold, an ice cube tray, or whatever is available) that has been moistened with a liquid detergent to prevent sticking.

Or roll the dough between two sheets of waxed paper and cut out forms with the wet edge of cookie cutters or molds. You can create some ornaments freehand, or without molds. Place screw eyes or ornament hooks into the ornaments while they are still wet. Set the ornaments aside to air dry. To speed up the drying process, you can place your ornaments in the oven, at 150°, for a short time. Check the directions on the material package.

"Instant" papier-mâché ornaments

STYROFOAM® BALL ORNAMENTS

The next time you visit a craft or artists' supply store, check their supply of Styrofoam®. It comes in sheets or squares that can be trimmed to various shapes. It also comes in preshaped forms. Two or more Styrofoam® pieces can be glued together with common white household glue (like Elmer's®). Push two or more straight pins through the pieces being joined to hold them tightly while the glue dries.

Once you have found the shape you want, or have made the figure of your choice, use white household glue to attach ribbons, sequins, buttons, and bows. Finish the ornament with a hook stuck into the top of the decoration and held firmly with a small dab of glue.

You can personalize your Styrofoam® ornaments by spelling out the names of various family members with buttons or sequins (available at fabric, department, and dime stores). Or you can glue small photographs on the ornaments. They make great Christmas gifts, too!

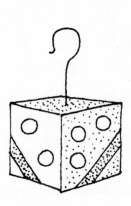

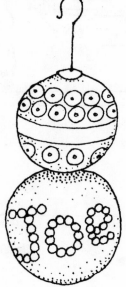

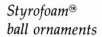

*Styrofoam®
ball ornaments*

8

THE MAGIC
OF CHRISTMAS

Over the centuries, thousands of Christmas stories have been written. Perhaps you have read some, yourself. Maybe you have a favorite one or two.

Yet, of all the tales that have been written, there is one—a verse—which continues to be the best-loved Christmas story of all time. It has been the subject of school plays. It has been the inspiration for short stories, cartoons, and movies. It has been put to music and recorded.

It is the story of the night before Christmas, by Clement C. Moore. It may be one of your all-time favorites, too. Here are the words.

A VISIT FROM SAINT NICHOLAS
BY CLEMENT C. MOORE

'Twas the night before Christmas, when all through the house
Not a creature was stirring, not even a mouse;

The stockings were hung by the chimney with care,
In hopes that Saint Nicholas soon would be there;
The children were nestled all snug in their beds,
While visions of sugarplums danced in their heads;
And mama in her kerchief, and I in my cap,
Had just settled our brains for a long winter's nap—
When out on the lawn there arose such a clatter,
I sprang from my bed to see what was the matter.
Away to the window I flew like a flash,
Tore open the shutters and threw up the sash.
The moon on the breast of the new-fallen snow
Gave a lustre of midday to objects below;
When what to my wondering eyes should appear,
But a miniature sleigh and eight tiny reindeer,
With a little old driver, so lively and quick,
I knew in a moment it must be Saint Nick!
More rapid than eagles his coursers they came,
And he whistled and shouted and called them by name:
"Now, Dasher! now Dancer! now, Prancer and Vixen!
On, Comet! on, Cupid! on, Donder and Blitzen!
To the top of the porch, to the top of the wall!
Now dash away, dash away, dash away all!"
As dry leaves that before the wild hurricane fly,
When they meet with an obstacle, mount to the sky,
So up to the housetop the coursers they flew,
With a sleigh full of toys—and Saint Nicholas, too.
And then in a twinkling I heard on the roof
The prancing and pawing of each little hoof.
As I drew in my head, and was turning around,
Down the chimney Saint Nicholas came with a bound.
He was dressed all in fur from his head to his foot,
And his clothes were all tarnished with ashes and soot;

A bundle of toys he had flung on his back,
And he looked like a peddler just opening his pack.
His eyes, how they twinkled! his dimples, how merry!
His cheeks were like roses, his nose like a cherry;
His droll little mouth was drawn up like a bow,
And the beard on his chin was as white as the snow.
The stump of a pipe he held tight in his teeth,
And the smoke it encircled his head like a wreath.
He had a broad face and a little round belly
That shook, when he laughed, like a bowl full of jelly.
He was chubby and plump—a right jolly old elf;
And I laughed, when I saw him, in spite of myself.
A wink of his eye and a twist of his head
Soon gave me to know I had nothing to dread.
He spoke not a word, but went straight to his work,
And filled all the stockings; then turned with a jerk,
And laying his finger aside of his nose,
And giving a nod, up the chimney he rose.
He sprang in his sleigh, to his team gave a whistle,
And away they all flew like the down of a thistle;
But I heard him exclaim, ere he drove out of sight:
"Merry Christmas to all, and to all a good-night!"

INDEX